KIRIGAMI

HOME DECORATIONS

Florence Temko

TUTTLE PUBLISHING
Tokyo • Rutland, Vermont • Singapore

First published in 2006 by Tuttle Publishing, an imprint of Periplus Editions (HK) Ltd., with editorial offices at 364 Innovation Drive, North Clarendon, Vermont 05759.

Library of Congress Cataloging-in-Publication Data
Temko, Florence.
 Kirigami home decorations / Florence Temko.
   p. cm.
 ISBN 0-8048-3793-7 (pbk.)
 1. Paper work. 2. Cut-out craft. I. Title.
 TT870.T4454 2004
 745.54—dc22   2004015745

Distributed by

North America, Latin America & Europe
Tuttle Publishing
364 Innovation Drive
North Clarendon, VT 05759-9436
Tel: (802) 773-8930
Fax: (802) 773-6993
Email: info@tuttlepublishing.com
www.tuttlepublishing.com

Japan
Tuttle Publishing
Yaekari Building, 3rd Floor
5-4-12 Ōsaki
Shinagawa-ku
Tokyo 141 0032
Tel: (03) 5437-0171
Fax: (03) 5437-0755
Email: tuttle-sales@gol.com

Asia Pacific
Berkeley Books Pte. Ltd.
130 Joo Seng Road
#06-01/03 Olivine Building
Singapore 368357
Tel: (65) 6280-1330
Fax: (65) 6280-6290
Email: inquiries@periplus.com.sg
www.periplus.com

First edition
09 08 07 06   10 9 8 7 6 5 4 3 2 1

Design by Linda Carey
Diagrams by Daniel P. Brennan based on original diagrams by Florence Temko
Photographs by Dave Kutchukian
Printed in Singapore

TUTTLE PUBLISHING ® is a registered trademark of Tuttle Publishing.

Contents

INTRODUCTION

Kirigami, the creative art of paper-cutting, is a surprisingly easy craft that requires only paper, a pair of scissors, and sometimes glue. In *Kirigami Home Decorations* you will find step-by-step directions for table centerpieces, wall pictures, flower bouquets, baskets, mobiles, and sculptures to brighten your home or fill up an odd corner.

For many designs a piece of paper is folded one or more times, with cuts added through all layers. When the paper is unfolded an unexpected symmetric design is revealed.

Cutting paper seems to be an instinctive pleasure. At an early age many children like to snip paper into small pieces. Before long they design pictures by pasting the shapes on a background. Papercutting is well recognized to provide educational benefits in the areas of art, math, graphic design, and hand-eye coordination. In *Kirigami Home Decorations* this experience has

been expanded for enjoyment by children as well as adults, who can achieve magic results with just a few cuts. My objective in writing *Kirigami Home Decorations* has been to provide projects that are simple to make, though they may look complex, and that will appeal to all ages.

KIRIGAMI QUESTIONS AND ANSWERS

Are origami and kirigami related?

As may be guessed, kirigami is related to origami, the art of folding paper.

Both words are translations from the Japanese and both include the Japanese word *gami*, which means "paper"; *ori* means "folding" and *kiri* means "cutting." In origami a paper square is folded into an object or animal without cutting or gluing. In

kirigami paper may be cut and glued, and may sometimes be folded before cutting. Many people find papercutting to be easier.

I popularized the word kirigami in the English language when I prepared a papercutting kit in 1962. At the time I had been practicing origami and

a publisher asked me to write a book about papercutting. When it came to choosing a title, the publishing staff and I sat around debating various possibilities. I suggested kirigami and we checked with the Japanese consulate to be sure this word would be acceptable. The kit had such a wide distribution that the word kirigami became a common term.

Are special scissors needed?

Any pair of scissors that feels comfortable is suitable for most of the designs in this book, but the sharper the better. If you move on to making intricate paper cuts, you may wish to acquire a pair of small scissors with narrow blades. Because paper contains silicones, which abrade scissors in time, it is best to reserve a pair of scissors especially for papercutting, since they may lose the sharpness needed for cutting fabric.

What kinds of papers are suitable?

Almost any kind of paper can be cut successfully. For a start use whatever is around the house, such as copy paper and gift wrap. Origami squares colored brilliantly on the front and white on the back are especially useful when paper has to be folded into several layers before cutting. For larger home decorations, card stock provides greater stability.

The selection of paper is one of the most important aspects of kirigami. When it comes to preparing beautiful objects, you may choose some more unusual papers, such as handmade

Japanese washi. Most cities now have a paper store with an interesting selection of papers from all over the world. Otherwise catalogs may prove helpful. And do not forget to recycle papers from flyers, magazines, and correspondence.

What are some of the practical uses for kirigami?

Obviously the title of this book, *Kirigami Home Decorations*, suggests some applications, but do not overlook adapting papercuts for party decorations, greeting cards, gift wrapping, school reports, and in other ways.

What about cards and gift wrapping?

The flat surfaces of cards, gift packages, and gift bags lend themselves to applying paper cuts, and are especially useful for mailing. It is a good idea to make a bunch of cutouts for cards or gift wrapping all at one time, ready for future birthdays or holidays. Nowadays, when what's outside the gift seems almost as important as the gift itself, kirigami ideas can help you create unusual packaging. It may even trump the contents when a recipient treasures one of your cards enough to frame it or keep a box for storing small items.

Remember that the selection of beautiful papers will always enhance your efforts and that many designs can be placed either vertically or horizontally as the card or box demands.

Is kirigami educational?

Definitely. Whether in the classroom or art room, working on some of the projects in this book will improve students' graphic design ability, color sense, and visual acuity. Some of the projects are based on geometry and help students visualize math concepts. In social studies students can investigate paper crafts as practiced in different countries.

Studies show that, among other benefits, papercutting improves manual dexterity by exercising and training small motor muscles, as well as furthering interaction between hand and mind. Most projects in this book are relevant for use in the classroom and can be related to curriculum requirements. In California papercutting is included in the "Framework for Public Schools, K–12."

At what age can children begin to cut paper?

With the availability of safety scissors, very young children can have fun cutting paper. In fact, it seems a natural outlet that can keep them occupied for long periods of time. Papercutting, like any craft, offers children and adults different challenges for different ages and different stages of development.

Is papercutting creative?

In a way papercutting is "drawing with scissors," so that taking a pair of scissors in hand invites limitless designing. Some artists who have applied their talents to paper-cutting have created true works of art. They may pencil in their design first, or they may work freehand. Since papercutting lends itself well to producing simple, dynamic, or bold images, it has been used in many advertisements and company logos. Some of these are based on Japanese crest cutting.

To explore your own creativity, experiment with

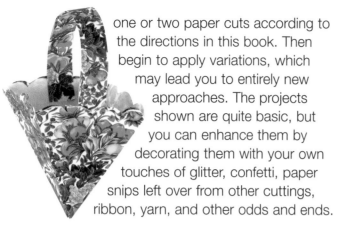

one or two paper cuts according to the directions in this book. Then begin to apply variations, which may lead you to entirely new approaches. The projects shown are quite basic, but you can enhance them by decorating them with your own touches of glitter, confetti, paper snips left over from other cuttings, ribbon, yarn, and other odds and ends.

What about copying the designs?

For some projects you may wish to follow the cutting lines exactly. You can copy the patterns by freehand drawing, tracing, photocopying, or computer scanning. Place the copy on top of the piece of paper you have selected and cut through all layers. For making more than one copy of a pattern, cut through several pieces of thin paper placed on top of each other. If you intend to make many copies, cut a template from strong paper that can be used over and over again.

It's all right to copy the designs for personal use, but not for any commercial applications.

PAPERCUTTING TECHNIQUES

Diagrams

The following symbols are used:

A line of this thickness shows the outline shape of the paper or existing creases made previously.

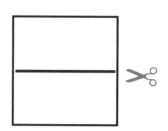

Cut on the heavier lines.

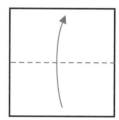

Fold toward you on the broken lines (valley fold).

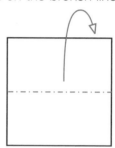

Fold away from you on the broken/dotted lines (mountain fold).

Square Paper

For some of the projects, square pieces of paper are indicated. You can cut any letter-size paper or other rectangle into a square with this simple method:

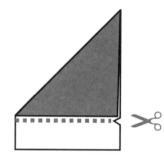

1. Fold a short edge to a long edge, bisecting a corner.
2. Cut off the extra rectangle.

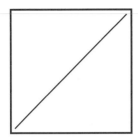

3. Completed square.

Measurements

Measurements are given in inches and centimeters, but they may not always be exactly equal in order to avoid awkward fractions. In some cases specific sizes are recommended, but in most cases you may use smaller or larger pieces of paper.

Scissors or Utility Knife?

All patterns can be cut with scissors. Many people, including me, are more comfortable with scissors than with craft knives. If you prefer, you can use a utility knife, which allows for more intricate cutting. Several layers can be cut at the same time by holding the knife like a chisel, straight down. In this case always use a board or a magazine for backing to avoid marring a tabletop or other surface.

How to Cut

When cutting curves, always hold the hand with the scissors still and move the paper into the scissors. Though it may seem awkward at first, this method will become a habit in a short time and will result in smoother cuts. Your paper cuts may not look exactly like the illustrations—scissors have a way of wanting to go their own way and you should let them.

Some artisans cut even very intricate designs with the shank of the scissors, which is the part of the blades closest to the handles. This provides better control. So why don't you try it and see how it works for you.

BUTTERFLY WINDOW PICTURE

For this cutout a piece of dark or gold paper is backed with colored tissue paper for a see-through effect.

You need:
Piece of letter paper
Dark color paper
Tissue paper in three colors
Pencil and tracing paper, photocopy, or computer scan
Scissors or craft knife
Glue stick
Small pieces of masking tape

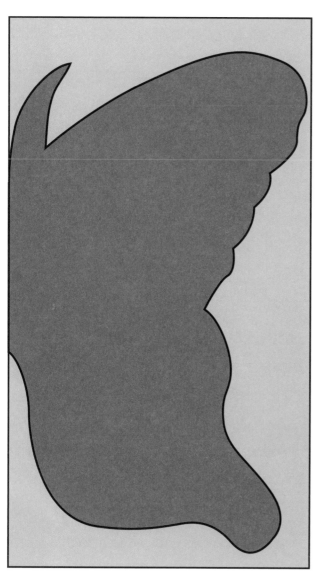

1. Draw, trace, photocopy, or scan half the butterfly.

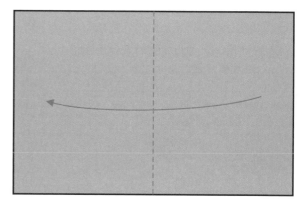

2. Fold another piece of dark paper in half.

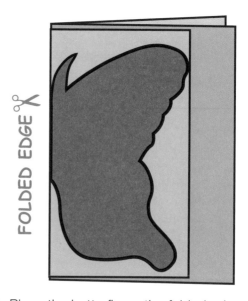

FOLDED EDGE

3a. Place the butterfly on the folded edge.
3b. Cut the outline through all layers.

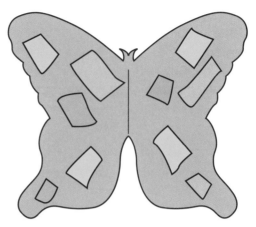

4a. Cut the interior areas either with scissors or a craft knife. If you're using scissors, first pierce a small hole in the middle of the area to be cut away. Insert the scissors and cut around on the lines. When using a craft knife, place the work on a magazine or other backing to protect the table surface from being nicked.

4b. Unfold the butterfly.

5a. Cut pieces of tissue paper to fit around the open areas.

5b. Paste them to the back of the butterfly.

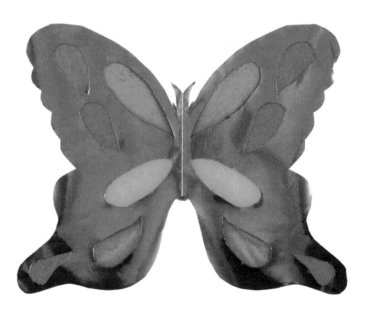

6. Completed Butterfly Window Picture. Paste the four corners against a window with small loops of masking tape.

LARGER BUTTERFLY

A larger size is easier to handle. The butterfly shown in the illustration was enlarged to a height of 10" (25 cm).

KIRIGAMI SUN

Kirigami is the widely practiced folk art of cutting paper into a great variety of designs that are often used as wall and window decorations. Use the cutout of a sun to brighten up days of dull weather.

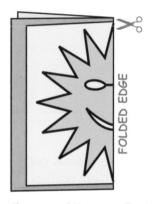

You need:
Colored paper
Pencil and tracing paper, photocopy, or computer scan
Scissors
Masking tape

1. Draw, trace, photocopy, or scan half the sun.

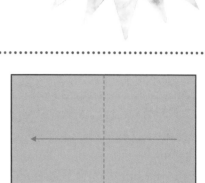

2. Fold another piece of paper in half.

FOLDED EDGE

3a. Place the half-copy of the sun flush with the folded edge of the paper.
3b. Cut on all the lines through all layers of paper.
3c. Unfold the sun. Note that the slit cut from the folded edge to the eye disappears.

4. Completed Kirigami Sun. Attach it to the window with a loop of masking tape.

FLOWER GARLANDS

Here is an effective way to decorate rooms and gyms. These garlands can be transported flat, which means they can be stored ahead of time and unfolded at another location for last-minute decorating.

Tissue paper usually comes in 30" x 20" (75 cm x 50 cm) sheets.

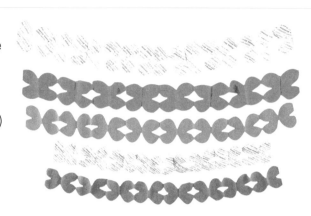

You need:
Tissue paper
Pencil
Scissors

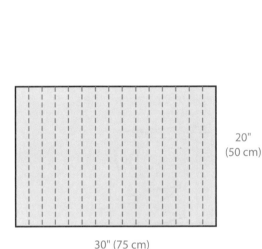

30" (75 cm)

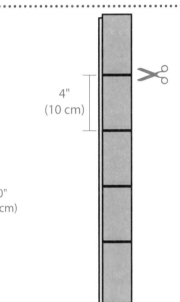

4"
(10 cm)

20"
(50 cm)

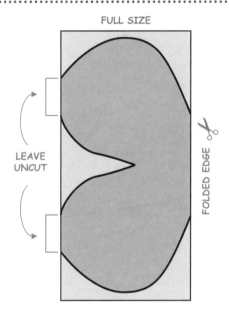

FULL SIZE

LEAVE
UNCUT

FOLDED EDGE

1. Fold a sheet of tissue paper in half four times, parallel to the shorter edges. You will have a bundle approximately 2" x 20" (5 cm x 50 cm).

2. Cut the bundle approximately 4" (10 cm) apart into five packets. Each packet makes one garland.

3a. Along the long edge, draw half of a flower as shown. Note that parts of both side edges are left intact, since otherwise the garland would fall apart.

3b. Cut on the lines.

3c. Unfold the paper.

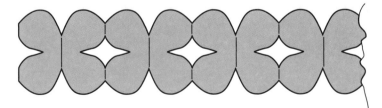

4. Completed Flower Garland.

LONGER GARLANDS

Glue or staple garlands end to end for longer chains.

WALL FLOWER

In China once a year, windows and walls are decorated with fresh paper cutouts called "Window Flowers," although the designs may include scenes from everyday life. Some patterns have been handed down from generation to generation. Parents and grandparents pass on the skill of papercutting with the result that some very intricate pictures have developed over a long period of time. Some have been used as stencils for embroidery patterns since the fifteenth century.

The window flower shown here can be cut by anyone. Lightweight papers, such as origami squares, are best.

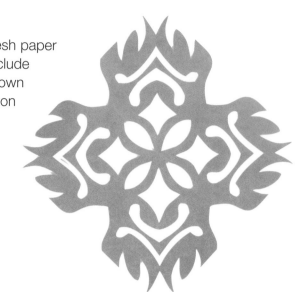

You need:
6" (15 cm) square of paper
Pencil and tracing paper, photocopy, or computer scan
Piece of letter paper
Scissors
Masking tape

PREFOLDING

In steps 1 through 3, follow the direction of the arrows carefully.

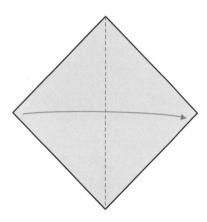

1. Fold the square from corner to corner.

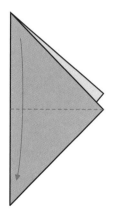

2. Fold it in half again.

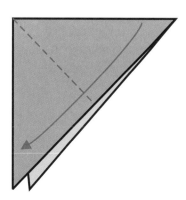

3. Fold the paper in half.

CLOSED CORNER

LAYERED CORNER IS HERE

4. You will have a triangle.

WALL FLOWER

CUTTING

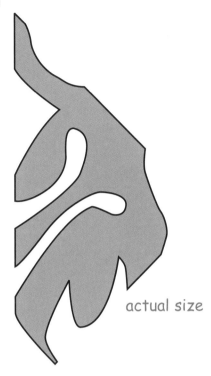

actual size

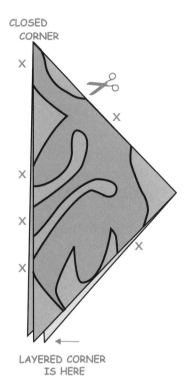

CLOSED CORNER

X
X
X
X
X
X

LAYERED CORNER
IS HERE

1. Draw, trace, photocopy, or scan the design on a piece of letter paper.

2a. Place it on the folded paper exactly as shown.

2b. Cut on the lines. Do not cut away sections of the edges marked with an X.

2c. Unfold the paper.

YOUR OWN DESIGNS

For the window flower you have folded a square of paper into a triangle and cut away sections from all three edges. None of the cuts go all the way from one edge to another, or the flower would fall apart. Once you understand this method you can cut your own designs freehand and probably enjoy unexpected results.

3. Completed Wall Flower. Paste the four corners against a window with small loops of masking tape.

PAPERED EGGS

Decorating eggs with pieces of paper napkins is a fun activity for families and other groups to add a special touch to a party at any time of the year, but especially at Easter.

Plastic eggs, hard-boiled eggs, or blown eggs may be used. Caution: Do not eat a hard-boiled egg after it has been decorated. To prepare a blown egg, carefully poke a small hole at each end and blow out the insides.

The papering is done in several steps, which do not take long. After each step the glue has to dry and you can do other things meanwhile, but the whole procedure may take several hours. The instructions begin with making a stand on which to hold the eggs while they are drying.

You need:
Stiff paper
Plastic, hard-boiled, or blown egg
Paper napkin with a small pattern
Small pieces of sponge
White glue
Plastic spoon

STAND

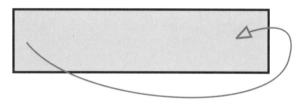

1. Cut a piece of stiff paper 5½" x ¾" (13 cm x 1.5 cm)

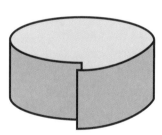

2a. Roll the strip around and glue both ends together.
2b. Completed Stand.

PAPERING AN EGG

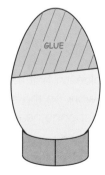

1. Wipe glue on half of an egg with a small piece of sponge. Let the glue dry until it is no longer milky and sticky, but clear and dry. This may take quite a while.

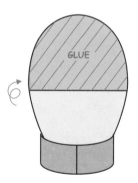

2. Turn the egg upside down and cover the other half with glue. Let it dry.

PAPERED EGGS

3. While the egg is drying, cut or (better still) tear out designs from a paper napkin. They can be motifs or random pieces. On double-layered napkins, use only the top layer.

4a. Wipe another coating of glue on one half of the egg. Carefully place the cutouts on it, smoothing them over with your fingers or a plastic spoon. Small wrinkles may appear. Let the egg dry again.

4b. Turn the egg upside down and repeat on the other half.

4c. Wipe on a final coat of glue on one half, and then on the other half when the first half is dry.

4d. Completed Papered Egg.

Tips

- Work on newspaper.
- All coats of white glue will dry transparent.
- For each coating, spread glue on half the egg; let it dry on a stand and then work on the other end.
- Have a moistened piece of sponge nearby to wipe glue off your fingers as you work.
- At each step you can tamp down the paper with the back of a plastic spoon.

BLOOMS

Paper blooms are a welcome touch for party decorating.

You need:
Colored paper for flower
Green paper for leaves
Compass or jar lid
Pencil
Floral wire or chenille stem
Scissors
Glue

BLOOM

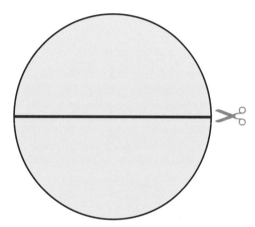

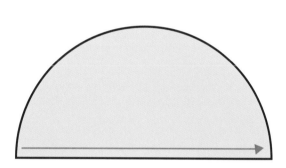

1a. Draw a circle about 2½" (5 cm) in diameter on the colored paper using a compass or jar lid and cut it out.

1b. Cut the circle in half. Each half will make a flower.

2. Roll the half-circle into a cone and glue the straight edges together.

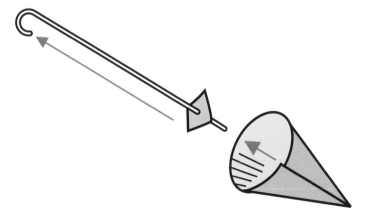

3a. Bend the end of the wire into a hook.

3b. Push a small scrap of the colored paper all the way up the wire and crush it around the hook. Then push the cone up over it.

BLOOMS

4a. Drop a little glue into the flower to hold it together.
4b. Completed bloom.

LEAVES

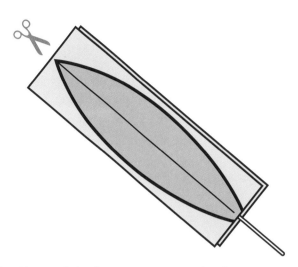

1a. For each leaf, cut two rectangles from green paper. Place the pieces together and insert a piece of wire in between.
1b. Glue the rectangles together.
1c. Taper the sides.

2. Completed Leaf.

3. Completed Blooms and Leaves.

FAKE CAKE TABLE CENTERPIECE

For one of my birthdays, a friend who couldn't celebrate with me in person sent me a fake cake decorated with silk flowers. I thought it was great fun and decided to simplify the idea and share it here.

You need:
Card stock
Colored paper
Compass or small plate
Pencil
Scissors
Glue
Ribbon
8" (20 cm) paper doily

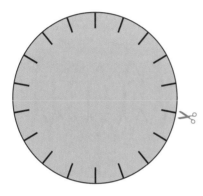

1a. Draw a circle with a 7" (18 cm) diameter on the card and cut it out.

1b. Cut ½" (1 cm) slits around the edge.

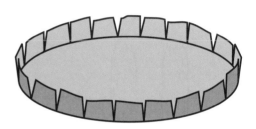

2. Bend up the notches at the edge of the circle.

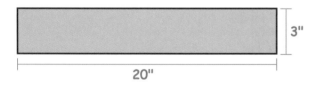

3"

20"

3. Cut a piece of card 20" x 3" (50 cm x 8 cm).

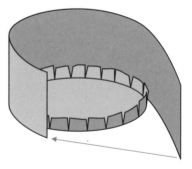

4a. Set the circle on a table with the notches facing up. Curve the long piece around and glue it to the notches.

4b. The ends of the long strip will overlap. Glue them together.

FAKE CAKE TABLE CENTERPIECE

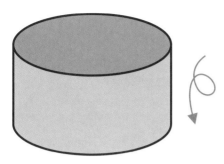

5. Turn the cake upside down.

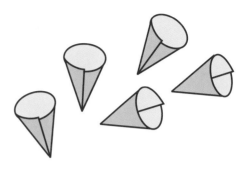

6. Make many blooms as described in the previous project.

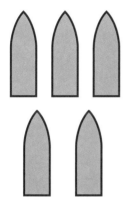

7. From green paper, cut many 2½" (7 cm) leaves with a curved top and a straight edge at the bottom.

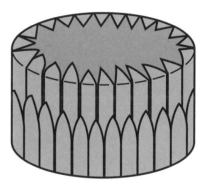

8. Glue the leaves to the sides of the cake in two layers. Bend and glue the top of one set of leaves over the edge of the cake.

9a. Glue the flowers on top.
9b. Glue on a ribbon bow.
9c. Set the cake on the paper doily.
9d. Completed Fake Cake Table Centerpiece.

Fish Mobile

The fish seem to be swimming in the sea when even a light air current moves this suspended mobile.

You need:
Printing paper in blue, red, green, and yellow
Pencil and tracing paper, photocopy, or computer scan
Pencil
Scissors
Glue
Needle and thread, or fishing line

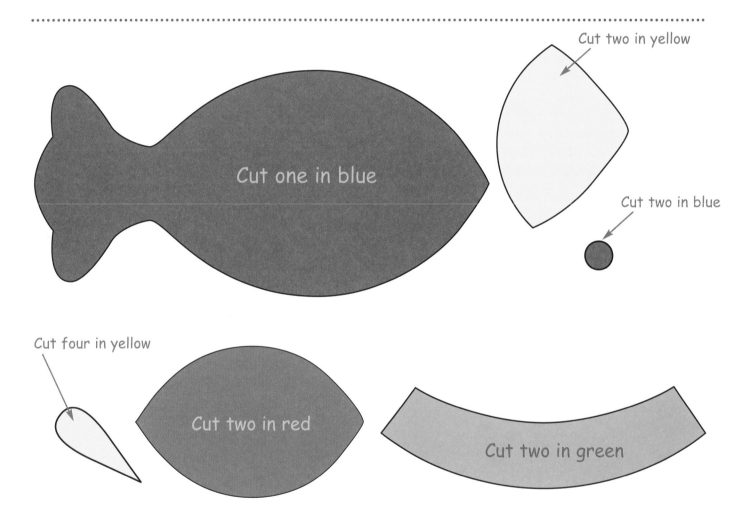

Cut two in yellow

Cut one in blue

Cut two in blue

Cut four in yellow

Cut two in red

Cut two in green

1a. Trace, photocopy, or scan the parts of the fish, shown full size.

1b. Place the copy on two pieces of the appropriate colored papers and cut out through all layers.

FISH MOBILE

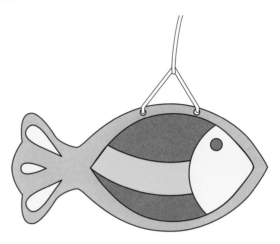

2a. Glue the pieces on the front and on the back of the fish in this order: a red piece on a blue fish, next the green piece on top, and finally the yellow pieces and the blue eye. Unless the pieces have been cut very accurately, you may want to shift them around and perhaps cut a snip off here and there.

2b. A completed fish.

3a. To suspend the fish, knot a loop of thread in two places. Attach another piece of thread to the loop for hanging. The fish can be shifted on the loop to balance it to hang evenly.

3b. Completed Fish Mobile.

MORE FISH

Use the tracings of the pieces again and again for making additional fish, which can be hung at different levels.

DIFFERENT SIZES

Enlarge or reduce the fish and interior pieces on a photocopy machine, or draw them freehand.

THREE FISH MOBILE

Suspend three fish one on top of another.

Five-pointed Star

Find out the secret how to cut a five-pointed star from a piece of paper with only one cut. With this method you can cut stars in any size, as long as you begin with a piece of paper in the proportion of 5 x 4.

You need:
Piece of paper 8" x 10" (20 cm x 25 cm)
Pencil
Scissors

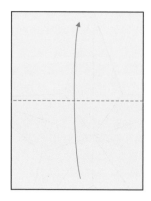

1. Fold the paper in half the short way.

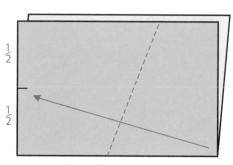

FOLDED EDGE

2a. Mark the middle of the short edge with a pencil.

2b. Place the paper with the folded edge toward you. Bring the right-hand corner to the mark on the opposite edge and crease.

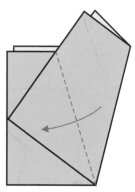

3. Fold the right edge over to the left and crease.

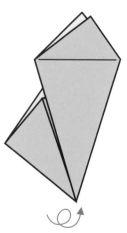

4. Turn the paper over.

22

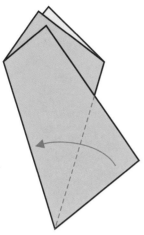

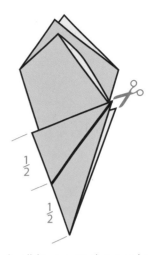

5. Fold the edge that is now on the right over to the left.

6. Cut through all layers at the angle shown.

$\frac{1}{2}$

$\frac{1}{2}$

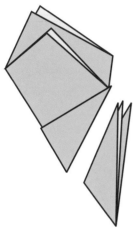

7. You will have two pieces of paper. Unfold the long triangle into a star.

8. Completed Five-Pointed Star.

3-D STAR

Fold a star up and down on alternate lines (mountain and valley folds). The angles of the points can be varied by changing the angle of the cut in step 6.

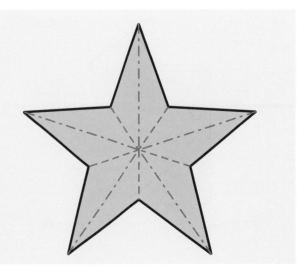

BIG BOLD CALENDAR

One time I received the gift of a wall calendar where each month was highlighted with a different illustration contributed by members of the same family. The original calendar was made with heavy, stiff handmade paper. When I decided to emulate the idea I used Canson Mi-Teintes because it comes in many colors. Construction or other heavy papers can be used instead.

You need:
12 pieces of card stock, 12" x 18" (30 cm x 45 cm)
Colored papers
Pencil and tracing paper, photocopy, or computer scan
Markers
Scissors
Glue
Hole punch

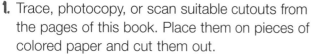

1. Trace, photocopy, or scan suitable cutouts from the pages of this book. Place them on pieces of colored paper and cut them out.

2a. Glue them on the upper half of the card stock, one design for each month. When you are pleased with the arrangements, glue them down.

2b. On the lower half of the card stock, write in the monthly dates with markers. You can also photocopy pages of a wall calendar and glue them on.

2c. Punch a hole at the top of the pages.

2d. Completed Big Bold Calendar.

GIFTS

Make photocopies of the calendar to give away.

CHERRY BLOSSOMS

Once you have mastered the basic folding procedure for the Five-Pointed Star you can adapt it to produce five-petalled flowers, which occur frequently in nature. Just think of cherry blossoms to celebrate the arrival of spring.

You need:
Pink copy paper 4" x 5" (10 cm x 12.5 cm)
Pencil
Scissors

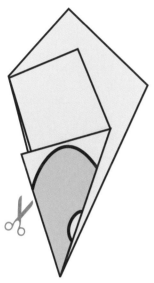

1a. Follow steps 1 through 5 for the Five-Pointed Star (see page 22).

1b. Make two rounded cuts, as shown, through all layers.

1c. Unfold the paper.

2. Completed Cherry Blossom.

SUN CATCHER

You can a make a semitransparent mobile with an arrangement of several cutouts, which is shown in the photo. The pieces are held in place between sheets of clear plastic, such as acetate page protectors. Attach a loop of thread at the top of the sun catcher.

THE FOUR SEASONS

Here are some suggestions for other designs for sun catchers:

- Rainbow: Cut arcs in the colors of the rainbow.
- Use other kirigami cutouts from this book and from other sources; for example, try an orange pumpkin for a jack-o'-lantern.

PHOTO PYRAMID

A pyramid showing family photos can be an admired table or desk decoration.

You need:
Cover stock or thin cardboard
Assorted photos
Pencil and tracing paper, photocopy, or computer scan
Scissors
Transparent tape
Glue

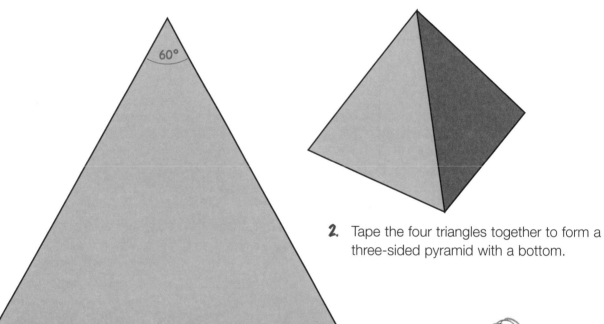

1a. Trace or photocopy the triangle (or draw an equilateral triangle with 60-degree corners).
1b. Place the tracing or photocopy on the card stock and cut out four triangles, one at a time.

2. Tape the four triangles together to form a three-sided pyramid with a bottom.

3a. Cut photos to fit on the triangles and glue them on the sides of the pyramid.
3b. Completed Photo Pyramid.

GIFT BOX

Make a pyramid but leave two "seams" on one triangle untaped to permit the box to open. To open the "door," staple or glue on a loop of ribbon.

SERVING BOWL

The choice of color and pattern is very important in making this serving bowl, as the construction itself could not be simpler.

You need:

Square of card stock, construction paper, or
      two pieces of gift wrap glued back to back
Scissors
Glue
Paper clips

1. Crease the square on both diagonals. Unfold each time.

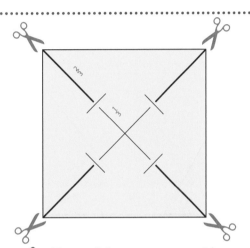

2. From all four corners, cut in about two-thirds on the creases.

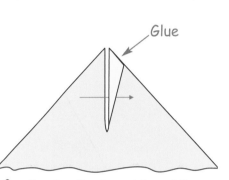

Glue

3. Overlap the two sides of the slits and glue them together. Hold them temporarily in place with paperclips until the glue has dried. Make sure there are no gaps at the end of the cuts near the bottom of the bowl.

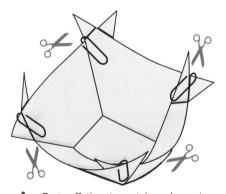

4. Cut off the two triangles at each corner that extend over the rim of the bowl.

5. Completed Serving Bowl.

WALLPAPER

A bowl will have a nice texture when it is made from two squares of wallpaper bonded together.

FRAME WITH EASEL

Decorative frames can be made by folding pieces of gift wrap paper in quarters and cutting away the interior. Select paper that complements the colors in the photograph you intend to frame.

The size given fits a 4" x 6" (10 cm x 15 cm) photograph. You can create frames to fit pictures in other sizes.

You need:
Gift wrap paper 6" x 8" (15 cm x 20 cm)
Card stock, 6" x 8" (15 cm x 20 cm)
Card stock 3" x 3" (8 cm x 8 cm)
Ruler
Pencil
Scissors
Glue

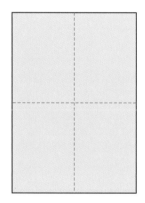

1. Fold the gift wrap paper into quarters.

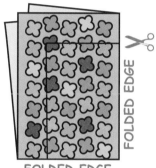

2a. Draw lines 1" (2.5 cm) parallel to the two outer edges that are not folded edges.
2b. Cut on the lines up to the point where they meet.
2c. Unfold the paper.
2d. Glue the outer piece onto the larger piece of card stock.

3. Completed frame.

FRAME WITH EASEL

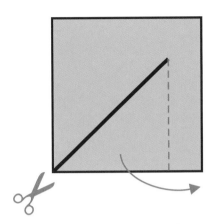

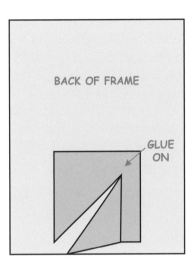

BACK OF FRAME

GLUE ON

4. Make an easel from the small square of card stock. Make a diagonal cut to form a notch and bend it outward.

5. Glue the easel to the back of the frame ¼" (½ cm) away from the bottom edge, but let the notch stick out.

6a. Glue on the photo or other image.
6b. Completed Frame with Easel.

FANCY EDGING

Before unfolding the paper, cut curved scallops or triangles along the outer edges.

HANGING PAGODA

It is hard to imagine that this elaborate ornament is made by "stretching" a paper square with a few well-placed cuts.

You need:
8" (20 cm) square of origami paper
1" (2 cm) square of card stock
Scissors
Needle and thread

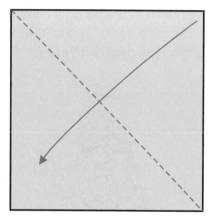

1. Fold the upper right corner of the square to the lower left corner.
Note: In steps 1–3 follow the direction of the arrows carefully.

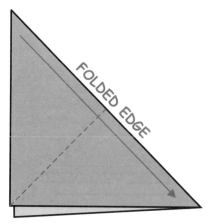

2. Fold the paper in half.

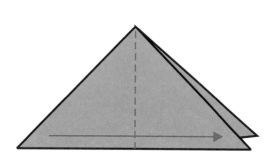

3. Fold it in half again. You will have a triangle.

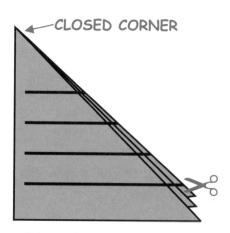

CLOSED CORNER

4. Make parallel cuts in from the longest edge, about ¾" (2 cm) apart and stopping about ¼" (½ cm) away from the opposite edge.

HANGING PAGODA

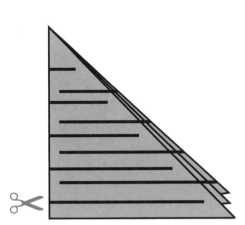

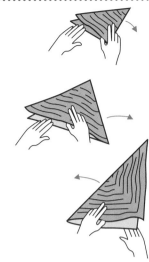

5. Now cut between the slits you just made, but cut toward the long edge. Again, stop about ¼" (½ cm) away from the edge.

6. Since the layers are inclined to lock at the slits, unfold the paper very carefully by reversing the earlier folding steps and restoring the original square.

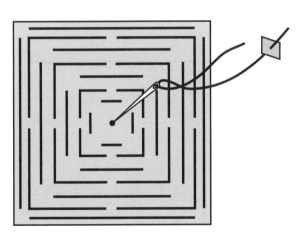

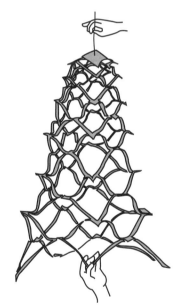

7a. Thread a needle and knot one end. Pass the needle through the small cardboard square and then through the center of the mobile from underneath.

7b. Remove the needle and gently pull down the sides of the paper The cardboard square is inside the pagoda.

8. Completed Hanging Pagoda.

Tips

- If the mobile does not hang properly you may be using paper that is too heavy.
- Sometimes it helps to pinch the middle of each side at the bottom between your thumb and forefinger (in other words, make a valley fold).
- The same pattern can be cut from a 5" (12 cm) square of foil gift wrap for a holiday tree ornament.

CHRISTMAS POSTER

The illustration shows an interactive Christmas tree poster. When anyone who walks by pulls on the bottom of the tree, it will expand to reveal a greeting and holiday gifts underneath.

The main effect is produced by folding a piece of heavy paper into a wedge and adding parallel cuts.

You need:

Green construction or similar weight paper, 9" x 12" (A4)
Small piece of gold paper
Piece of paper
Poster board (or similar), 16" x 20" (40 cm x 50 cm)
Scissors
Marker
Glue

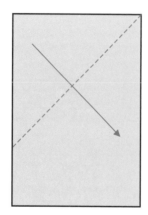

1. On the construction paper, fold a short edge to a long edge.

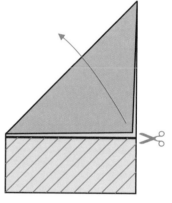

2. Cut off the extra rectangle. You will have a triangle.

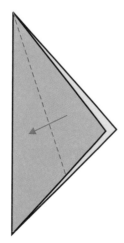

3. Fold one of the short edges to the long edge.

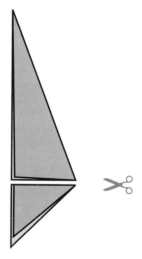

4. Cut straight across, as shown.

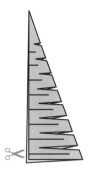

5. Make parallel cuts from one edge of the paper, but do not cut all the way across.

6a. Make parallel cuts from the opposite edge of the paper. Again, do not cut all the way across.

6b. Unfold the paper carefully.

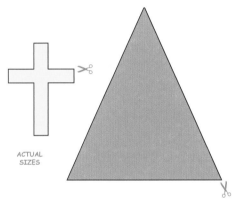

ACTUAL SIZES

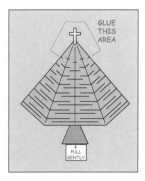

GLUE THIS AREA

PULL GENTLY

7a. Cut a small cross from gold paper.

7b. Cut a triangle for a tree trunk.

8a. Glue the cross and the top of the tree firmly on the poster board.

8b. On a small scrap of paper write "Pull Gently" and add an arrow. Glue it below the tree trunk on the poster board.

MERRY CHRISTMAS!

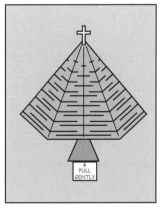
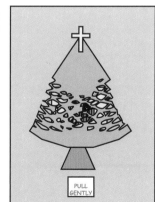

PULL GENTLY

PULL GENTLY

9a. Cut a piece of paper 5" x 3" (12 cm x 8 cm). Write "Merry Christmas!" on it (or other greeting) and draw on some gift boxes.

9b. Glue the message on the poster board behind the tree. Position it so that when you pull on the bottom of the tree the gifts appear.

10. Completed Christmas Poster.

MAY BASKET

For a festive occasion, fill several of these hanging baskets with dried flowers or candy. Sturdy paper, with or without a pattern, is best. You can use a plate or a compass for drawing the circle. A 10" (25 cm) diameter circle results in a 4" (10 cm) basket, measured without the handle.

You need:
Sturdy paper
Compass or plate
Pencil
Scissors
Stapler
Glue

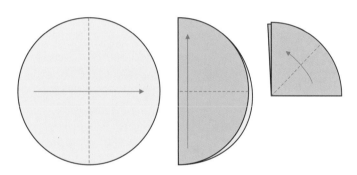

1a. Draw a circle on the paper and cut it out.
1b. Fold it in half three times.

2a. You will have a wedge. Cut scallops on the rounded edge through all layers.
2b. Unfold the paper. You will have a circle divided into eighths.

3a. If the paper is colored on one side only, place the white side up.
3b. Mountain fold A to B.
3c. Mountain fold C to D.

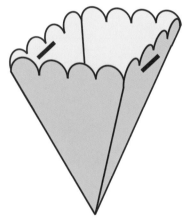

4. You will have a cone. Staple the multilayered sections together.

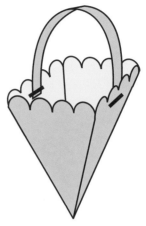

5a. Cut a strip of paper.

5b. Fold it in half lengthwise and glue it together.

5c. Staple the strip to the multilayered sections.

6. Completed May Basket.

PAPER QUILT: BASKET

Quilting strong graphic designs on bedspreads has been a creative outlet for several centuries. The same technique can be applied to producing paper quilts for dramatic wall hangings and in much less time.

The instructions show how to make a classic basket design using only right-angle triangles, also called Half Squares.

You need:

Colored printing paper or gift wrap in two colors
15" (38 cm) square card stock or poster board
Ruler
Pencil
Scissors
Glue stick

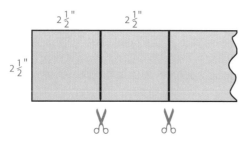

1a. Cut six 2½" (6 cm) squares from one color.

1b. Cut three 2½" (6 cm) squares from the other color.

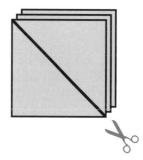

2. Cut all squares from corner to corner. You will have 12 triangles.

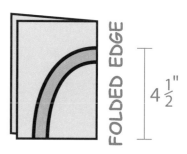

3a. Fold a piece of paper of the first color in half and cut out half a handle.

3b. Unfold it.

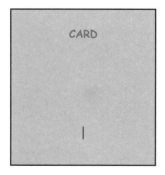

4. Lightly mark the middle of the piece of card.

5a. Arrange the triangles and the handle on the card as shown, building up from the bottom.

5b. Glue the triangles and handle on the card.

5c. Completed Basket Quilt.

FRIENDSHIP QUILTS

To commemorate special occasions such as a wedding or relocation of a colleague, have family members or friends inscribe individual pieces of the paper quilts with their name or a message. This can be done with the personal handwriting of each contributor or one person can sign them all for greater uniformity. Such a thoughtful gift will always recall precious memories for the recipient. It is advisable to choose plain light colors for the patches that are to be signed.

PAPER QUILT: TUMBLING BLOCKS

A popular quilting pattern called "Tumbling Blocks" creates an optical illusion. When you look at it intensely the blocks seem to fall forward one minute and fall backward the next minute. This phenomenon relies on a combination of three contrasting colors.

You need:
Colored printing or gift wrap in three colors
Card stock or poster board
Ruler
Pencil
Scissors
Glue stick

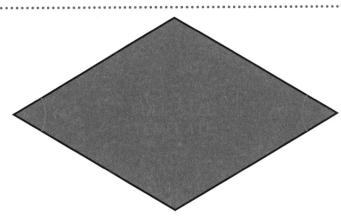

1. Copy the diamond with 60-degree angles on card stock or stiff paper and cut it out. This will be your template.

2a. From all three colors cut strips of paper 1½" (3.5 cm) wide.

2b. Place the template at one end of each strip and draw the two angled lines with the aid of the template.

3a. Repeat this procedure all along the strip, by moving the template along.

3b. Cut on all the angled lines. You will have many diamonds.

4a. Arrange the diamonds in the exact pattern shown and glue them down carefully on the card stock.

4b. Completed Tumbling Blocks Quilt. Trim the outside edges of the card as desired.

EXPERIMENT

Many quilts are based on simple geometric forms, such as squares, triangles, and diamonds, yet they can be arranged in hundreds of varying patterns. For example, you can have great fun arranging these diamonds into stars and other formations by relying on different placements and choice of colors.

ANGEL

The angel is cut and shaped from a single piece of paper.
Besides using it as an ornament, why not give it as a
reward to someone for being an angel.

You need:
Paper
Pencil and tracing paper, photocopy, or computer scan
Scissors
Transparent tape
Glue

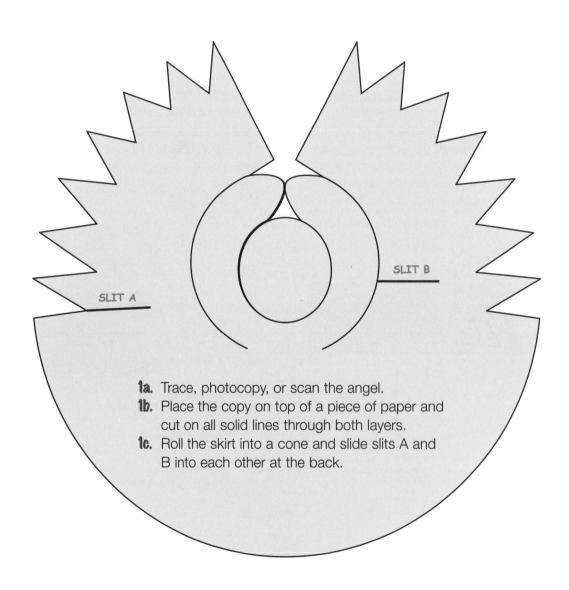

SLIT A

SLIT B

1a. Trace, photocopy, or scan the angel.
1b. Place the copy on top of a piece of paper and
cut on all solid lines through both layers.
1c. Roll the skirt into a cone and slide slits A and
B into each other at the back.

ANGEL

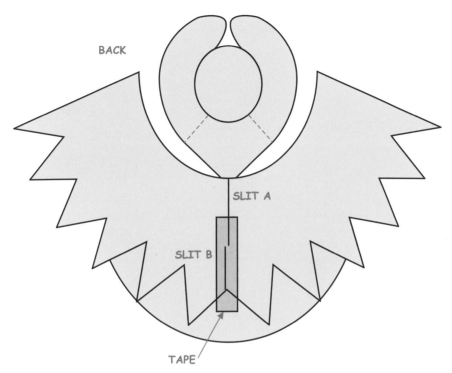

BACK

SLIT A

SLIT B

TAPE

2a. Adjust the position of the wings to suit you. Hold them in place with a piece of tape where the slits meet.

2b. Bend the arms to the front and glue the hands together. Bend the head forward a little.

3. Completed Angel.

TREASURE BOX

This box has a long tradition that vouches for its popularity and usefulness. It can be made from a square of any size.

You need:
Paper square
Scissors

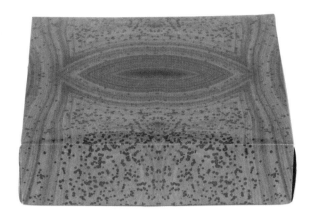

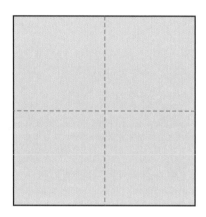

1. Fold the square in half in both directions. Unfold both times.

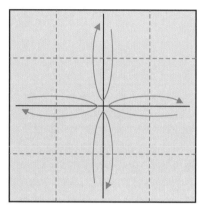

2. Fold the four edges to the middle creases. Unfold each time.

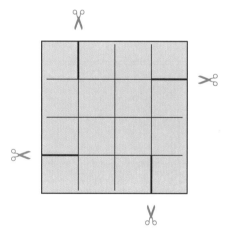

3. Make four cuts exactly as shown, always one square in from the edge on the right.

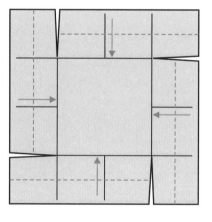

4. Fold the four edges to the nearest creases.

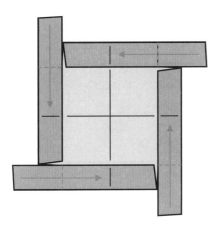

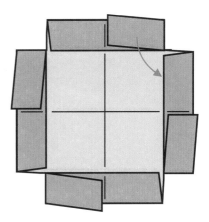

5. Fold the pieces that extend out, exactly as shown.

6a. Stand two adjacent edges straight up, making a corner.

6b. Tuck the extension piece under the nearest doubled edge, thereby locking the corner.

6c. Repeat with the other three corners.

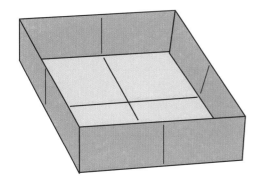

7. Completed Treasure Box.

BOX WITH A LID

For making a box with a lid you need two squares of paper, one of them ¼" (½ cm) smaller than the other. Fold both squares in the same way.

THE PROWLER

You will find many occasions for displaying the amusing prowler in your own home, to give as a present, or for illustrating a story. The Prowler is cut from stiff paper or card stock. It can be expanded into very large sizes for dramatic effects.

You need:
Card stock
Pencil and
    paper
Scissors
Marker

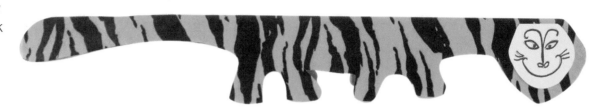

1. Copy the diagram of the Prowler as large as you like.

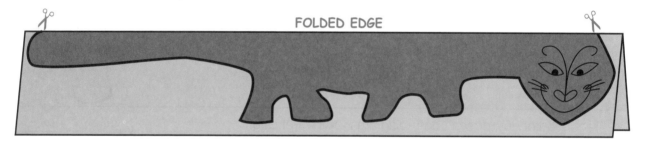

FOLDED EDGE

2a. Fold a piece of card in half. Place the diagram with the back of the Prowler along the folded edge.
2b. Cut on the outlines through all layers.
2c. Draw on the face with marker.

3. Completed Prowler.

PARTY GAME

Provide guests with the necessary materials and let them invent all kinds of stand-up animals, either by drawing them freehand or copying pictures from magazines, books, or the Internet. Some quite comic creatures may come to life.

THE PET DOG

The Pet Dog is a stand-up animal made up of two pieces. After you have followed the directions and understand the method, you can try to invent other animals, either by drawing them freehand or copying pictures from magazines, books, or the Internet.

You need:
Card stock
Pencil and tracing paper, photocopy,
    or computer scan
Scissors

Folded Edge

Cut a Slit Here

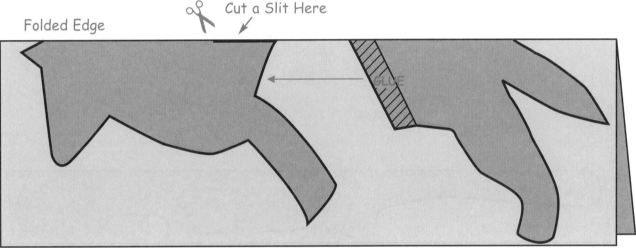

GLUE

1a. Trace, photocopy, or scan both diagrams for the Pet Dog.

1b. Cut a slit as shown.

1c. Fold a piece of card in half. Place the backs of both pieces of the dog along the folded edge and cut out.

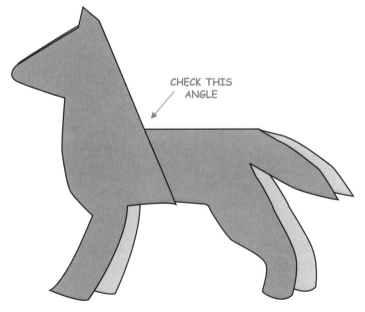

CHECK THIS ANGLE

2a. Glue or tape the two pieces together. To find the best angle for the dog to stand, check your paper against the angle in the illustration.

2b. Completed Pet Dog.

Football Player

When you hang the football player on the wall and pull the string, he will jump into action.

You need:
Card stock
Pencil and tracing paper, photocopy, or computer scan
Scissors
Large needle
4 double-pronged paper fasteners

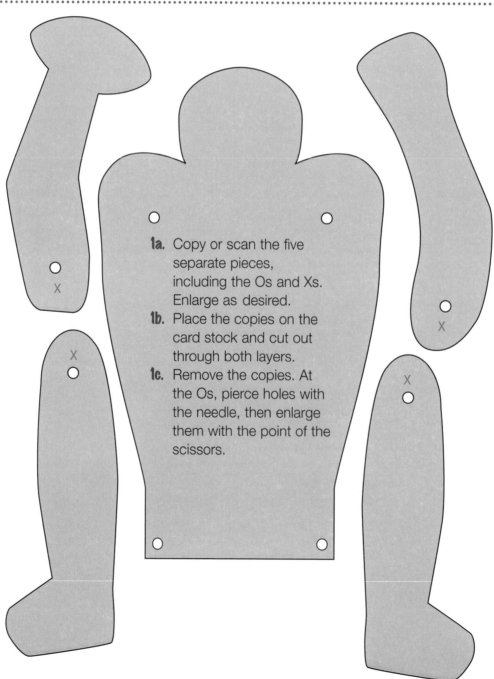

1a. Copy or scan the five separate pieces, including the Os and Xs. Enlarge as desired.

1b. Place the copies on the card stock and cut out through both layers.

1c. Remove the copies. At the Os, pierce holes with the needle, then enlarge them with the point of the scissors.

FOOTBALL PLAYER

Back

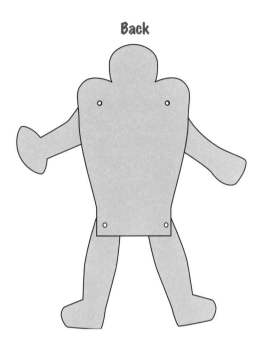

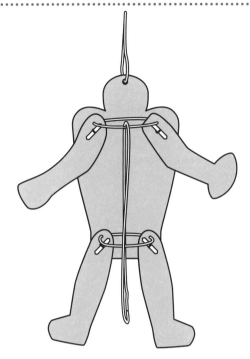

2. Attach the arms and legs behind the body with the paper fasteners through the O holes, spreading them apart in the back. Make sure the pieces move easily, but if not, loosen the fasteners.

3a. Let the limbs hang straight down at the sides. Knot a piece of thread between the Xs on the arms. Thread the legs together in the same way. (You can keep the limbs pointing down by taping a small weight on the back, such as a penny or a washer.)

3b. Knot a piece of thread to the middle of the arm and leg loops, letting it extend down a few inches.

3c. Attach a piece of thread to the hole at the top of the head.

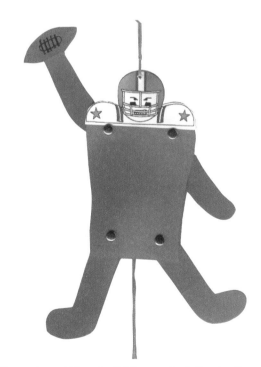

4. Completed Football Player. Pull the bottom thread to make the football player spring into action.

DECORATION

You can decorate the football player with the colors of your favorite team, or use photos of family members or illustrations of celebrities cut from magazine pages.

NAPKIN RINGS

For an unusual table setting, decorate simple paper bands with holly or any other cutouts in this book.

You need:
Green, yellow, and red printing papers
Pencil
Scissors
Glue

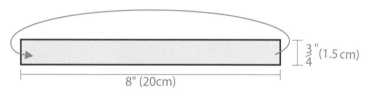

1a. Cut a piece of green or red paper 8" x ¾" (20 cm x 1.5 cm).

1b. Roll the strip around and glue both ends together.

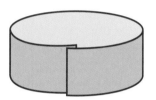

2. Completed ring.

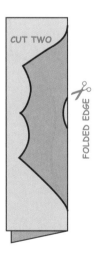

CUT TWO

FOLDED EDGE

3. Fold two pieces of green paper in half. Draw half a holly leaf on the folded edge. Cut out through all layers.

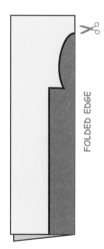

FOLDED EDGE

4. Fold a piece of red paper in half. Draw half a candle on the folded edge. Cut out through both layers.

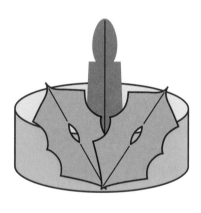

5a. Unfold the cutouts and glue them to the ring.

5b. Completed Napkin Ring.

PLACE CARDS

These simple place cards can be decorated with any cutout suited to the occasion. Their height will add interest to any table setting.

You need:
6" (15 cm) square of colored printing paper
Pencil and tracing paper, photocopy, or
    computer scan
Piece of light brown paper
Scissors
Glue
Black marker

1. Fold the square into quarters.

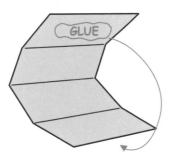

2. Overlap the two end sections and glue them together, forming a triangle.

3. Completed holder.

4a. Trace or copy half of the ▶ guitar.
4b. Fold the brown paper in half.
4c. Place the copy of the guitar on the folded edge of the paper and cut out through all layers.

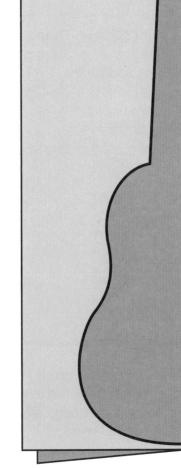

FOLDED EDGE

5a. Unfold the guitar and draw on strings.
5b. Glue the guitar to the holder.
5c. Completed Place Card.

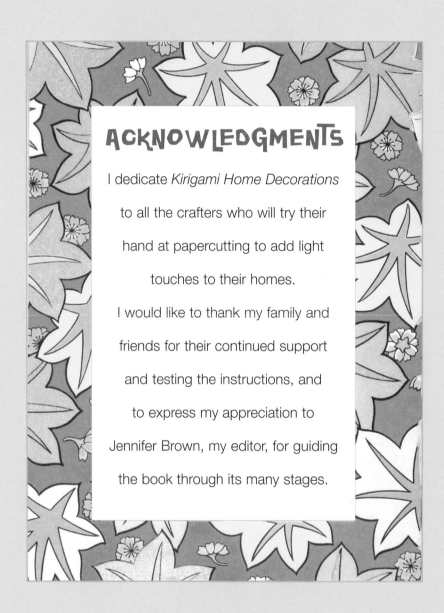

ACKNOWLEDGMENTS

I dedicate *Kirigami Home Decorations*

to all the crafters who will try their

hand at papercutting to add light

touches to their homes.

I would like to thank my family and

friends for their continued support

and testing the instructions, and

to express my appreciation to

Jennifer Brown, my editor, for guiding

the book through its many stages.